This is the story of:

_____

Written with love by:

_____

Date:

_____

Precious Little One

A Baby's Book
of the First Five Years

Erika J. MacArthur

ILLUSTRATIONS BY LAURIE JORDAN

CROSSWAY BOOKS · WHEATON ILLINOIS
A DIVISION OF GOOD NEWS PUBLISHERS

This is dedicated to my children,
Kylee Emelia, Andrew Fullerton and Brooke Lillian.
And to my husband Mark. I thank God for you always.

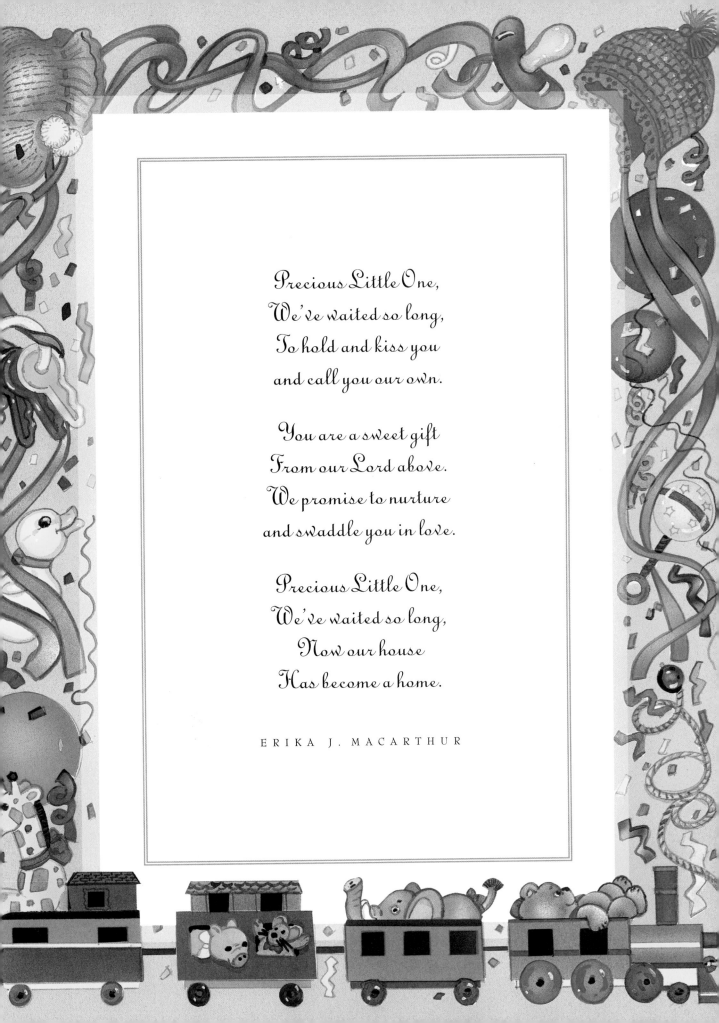

Precious Little One,
We've waited so long,
To hold and kiss you
and call you our own.

You are a sweet gift
From our Lord above.
We promise to nurture
and swaddle you in love.

Precious Little One,
We've waited so long,
Now our house
Has become a home.

ERIKA J. MACARTHUR

Waiting for You

For Thou didst form my inward parts;
Thou didst weave me in my mother's womb.

PSALM 139:13

The Good News

Our first reaction to the news _____

_____

_____

How we celebrated _____

_____

_____

The first people we told _____

_____

_____

Advice from family and friends _____

_____

_____

How we prepared for your arrival _____

_____

_____

Special things baby inherited _____

_____

_____

Special Thoughts for You

With all our love, _____

Family Tree

PATERNAL

_____

great grandfather

_____

birthplace, date

_____

great grandmother

_____

birthplace, date

_____

grandfather

_____

birthplace, date

_____

great grandfather

_____

birthplace, date

_____

great grandmother

_____

birthplace, date

_____

grandmother

_____

birthplace, date

_____

father

_____

birthplace, date

And Jesus said, "I am the vine, you are the branches; he who

Family Tree

MATERNAL

_____
great grandfather

_____
birthplace, date

_____
great grandmother

_____
birthplace, date

_____
grandfather

_____
birthplace, date

_____
great grandfather

_____
birthplace, date

_____
great grandmother

_____
birthplace, date

_____
grandmother

_____
birthplace, date

_____
mother

_____
birthplace, date

abides in Me, and I in him, he bears much fruit." —JOHN 15:5

My Parents

PHOTO OF CHILD'S PARENTS HERE

My Photo

BABY'S ULTRASOUND PHOTO

My Mother's Parents

PHOTO OF MOTHER'S PARENTS HERE

My Father's Parents

PHOTO OF FATHER'S PARENTS HERE

All About Mother

Mother's full name _____

When and where she was born _____

Where she grew up _____

Her brothers, sisters and their birthdays _____

_____

Her education _____

Her occupation _____

Her special interests and hobbies _____

Special childhood memories _____

Her favorite Bible verse _____

How we met _____

When and where we were married _____

For the Lord is good; His Loving kindness is everlasting,

All About Father

Father's full name _____

When and where he was born _____

Where he grew up _____

His brothers, sisters and their birthdays _____

_____

His education _____

His occupation _____

His special interests and hobbies _____

Special childhood memories _____

His favorite Bible verse _____

Special memories from our wedding day _____

_____

and His faithfulness to all generations. —PSALM 100:5

All about Mother's Parents

Grandmother's full name _____

When and where she was born _____

Her special interests and talents _____

_____

Grandfather's full name _____

When and where he was born _____

His special interests and hobbies _____

Where and when they were married _____

_____

Family traditions passed down _____

Their favorite Bible verse _____

All about Father's Parents

Grandmother's full name _____

When and where she was born _____

Her special interests and talents _____

_____

Grandfather's full name _____

When and where he was born _____

His special interests and hobbies _____

Where and when they were married _____

Family traditions passed down _____

_____

Their favorite Bible verse _____

Before Baby was Born

Showers given by   Where, when

_____   _____

_____   _____

_____   _____

_____   _____

Special gifts _____

_____

_____

Special memories _____

_____

_____

"As you enter the house, give it your greeting," said Jesus.

MATTHEW 10:12

Baby is on the Way

How baby's name was chosen _____

_____

Other names considered _____

_____

Notes about pregnancy _____

_____

_____

What parents were doing when contractions began _____

_____

Trip to the hospital _____

_____

_____

Rejoice in the Lord Always; Again I will say rejoice!

PHILIPPIANS 4:4

Your Arrival

Children are a gift from the Lord.

PSALM 127:3

Footprint

Date _____

Handprint

Date _____

Jesus loves the little children, all the children of the world. Red and yellow, black and white, they are precious in His sight. Jesus loves the little children of the world. His sight. Jesus loves the little children of the world. Red and yellow, black and white, they are precious in His sight.

Our Precious Gift

BABY'S PHOTO HERE

Baby's Birth

Date _____   Time _____   Place _____

Weight _____   Length _____   Blood type _____

Eye color _____   Hair color _____

Baby resembles _____

_____

Who was there _____

_____

Mom's first reaction _____

_____

_____

Dad's first reaction _____

_____

_____

Nurse's name _____

Doctor's name _____

Announcing Your Arrival

PLACE BABY'S ANNOUNCEMENT HERE

*"Dear Little One, Our Prayer for You is that You...
...Shall Love the Lord Your God with all Your Heart and with
all Your Soul and with all Your Might."*

DEUTERONOMY 6:5

The World Around Baby

Weather _____

Local news _____

_____

World news _____

_____

World leaders _____

Hit Songs _____

_____

Best-selling books _____

_____

Fads and fashions _____

_____

And do not be conformed to this world,
but be transformed by the renewing of your mind,
that you may prove what the will of God is,
that which is good and acceptable and perfect.

ROMANS 12:2

Baby's First Visitors

_____   _____

_____   _____

_____   _____

_____   _____

_____   _____

_____   _____

_____   _____

_____   _____

_____   _____

_____   _____

_____   _____

_____   _____

Beloved, let us love one another, for Love is from God;
and everyone who loves is born of God and knows God.

1 JOHN 4:7

Baby's First Home

PLACE PICTURE OF BABY'S

FIRST HOME HERE

As for me and my house, we will serve the Lord

JOSHUA 24:15

Homecoming

Date of arrival _____

Who brought baby home _____

What baby wore _____

Home address _____

Who was waiting to greet you _____

_____

What the nursery looked like _____

_____

Our first night _____

_____

_____

Brothers and sisters waiting _____

_____

Baby's Keepsakes

PLACE AN ENVELOPE HERE

FOR BABY'S KEEPSAKES

Include things like:
Baby's birth certificate
Baby's hospital tags
A lock of baby's hair

Growing Strong

You, however,
continue in the things you have learned and become convinced of,
knowing from whom you have learned them...
...and that from childhood you have known the sacred writings which
are able to give you the wisdom that leads to salvation
through faith which is in Christ Jesus.

II TIMOTHY 3:14-15

Baby's Firsts

Smiles _____

Laughs out loud _____

Sits up _____

Reaches for objects _____

Discovers feet _____

Crawls _____

Claps hands _____

Plays peekaboo _____

Holds cup _____

Eats solid food _____

Stands alone _____

Takes first steps _____

Walks alone _____

First tooth _____

First words _____

Baby's Firsts

Holds head up _____

Rolls over _____

Sleeps though the night _____

Gives kisses _____

Waves bye-bye _____

First overnight _____

Baby's First Haircut

PLACE PHOTO OF BABY'S

FIRST HAIRCUT HERE

Baby's Favorites

Stories _____

Songs _____

Games _____

Toys _____

Food _____

Places _____

_____

Mannerisms & Sayings _____

_____

Friends _____

_____

Family Members _____

_____

Caregivers _____

Baby's Growth

Date	Height	Weight	Comments

Photo of Baby's Dedication

Jesus kept increasing in wisdom and stature,
and in favor with God and men.

LUKE 2:52

Baby's Dedication to the Lord

Where dedication took place _____

Date _____

Those who were there _____

_____

_____

God Parents _____

Pastor _____

Note from pastor _____

_____

_____

_____

His intent was now, through the church, the manifold wisdom of God
should be made known to the rulers and authorities in the heavenly realms,
according to his eternal purpose which he accomplished in Christ Jesus our Lord.

EPHESIANS 3:10-11

Photos of Baby's First Birthday

Baby's First Birthday

PLACE BIRTHDAY PHOTO HERE

Where _____ When _____

Guests _____

_____

Decorations _____

_____

How we celebrated _____

_____

Baby's autograph _____

 # Second Birthday

PLACE BIRTHDAY PHOTO HERE

Where _____   When _____

Guests _____

_____

Decorations _____

_____

How we celebrated _____

_____

Baby's autograph _____

Third Birthday

PLACE BIRTHDAY PHOTO HERE

Where _____ When _____

Guests _____

_____

Decorations _____

_____

How we celebrated _____

_____

Baby's autograph _____

 # Fourth Birthday

PLACE BIRTHDAY PHOTO HERE

Where _____ When _____

Guests _____

_____

Decorations _____

_____

How we celebrated _____

_____

Baby's autograph _____

Fifth Birthday

PLACE BIRTHDAY PHOTO HERE

Where _____ When _____

Guests _____

_____

Decorations _____

_____

How we celebrated _____

_____

Baby's autograph _____

Sunday School Days

NURSERY

Teacher _____

Favorite song or activity _____

_____

Things most learned _____

_____

Finally brethren,
whatever is true, whatever is honorable,
whatever is right, whatever is pure, whatever is lovely,
whatever is of good repute,
if there is any excellence and if anything
worthy of praise, think on these things.

PHILIPPIANS 4:8

Sunday School Days

TWO YEAR OLD

Teacher _____

Favorite song or activity _____

_____

Things most learned _____

_____

THREE YEAR OLD

Teacher _____

Favorite song or activity _____

_____

Things most learned _____

_____

Sunday School Days

FOUR YEAR OLD

Teacher _____

Favorite song or activity _____

_____

Things most learned _____

_____

FIVE YEAR OLD

Teacher _____

Favorite song or activity _____

_____

Things most learned _____

_____

Our God is an awesome God. He reigns from heaven above with wisdom, power and love. Our God is an awesome God!

PLACE A DRAWING
OF WHAT GOD MEANS TO YOU.

First Day of School

PHOTO OF FIRST DAY OF SCHOOL

School Days

Name of School _____

Name of teacher _____

Friends _____

_____

First reaction _____

_____

Memories _____

_____

_____

_____

_____

_____

Special Friends

PHOTO OF SPECIAL FRIENDS

Special Memories _____

_____

_____

_____

_____

A Friend loves at all times.

PROVERBS 17:17

Our Family

PHOTO OF FAMILY

Family Traditions _____

_____

_____

_____

Special Memories _____

_____

_____

_____

Baby's First Christmas

"Glory to God in the highest,
and on earth peace among men with whom He is pleased."

LUKE 2:11-14

PHOTO OF

BABY'S FIRST CHRISTMAS

Special memories _____

_____

_____

_____

Christmas Memories

TWO YEAR OLD

Date _____ Where _____

Who was there _____

_____

Special memories _____

_____

THREE YEAR OLD

Date _____ Where _____

Who was there _____

_____

Special memories _____

_____

Christmas Memories

FOUR YEAR OLD

Date _____ Where _____

Who was there _____

_____

Special memories _____

_____

FIVE YEAR OLD

Date _____ Where _____

Who was there _____

_____

Special memories _____

_____

Our Hope For You

The law of the Lord is perfect,
restoring the soul;
The testimony of the Lord is sure,
making wise the simple.
The precepts of the Lord are right,
rejoicing the heart
The commandment of the Lord is pure,
enlightening the eyes.
The fear of the Lord is clean,
enduring forever;
The judgments of the Lord are true;
they are righteous altogether...
...in keeping them there is great reward.

PSALM 19:7-9, 11 (B)

Our Hope For You

MOTHER'S HOPE

_____

_____

_____

_____

With all my love, _____

FATHER'S HOPE

_____

_____

_____

_____

With all my love, _____

Your Salvation

Where, when _____

_____

_____

Most influential person(s) _____

_____

Your Testimony _____

_____

_____

_____

Jesus said to him,
"I am the way, and the truth,
and the life; no one comes to father, but through Me."

JOHN 14:6

Your Testimony continued _____

_____

_____

_____

_____

_____

_____

_____

_____

_____

_____

Your favorite verse(s) _____

_____

Your favorite pastor/preacher/teacher(s) _____

_____

Your Baptism

Where, when _____

_____

Name of pastor _____

Family & friends who were there _____

_____

_____

Special memories _____

_____

_____

How I felt _____

_____

_____

*Therefore we have been buried with Him through baptism into death,
in order that as Christ was raised from the dead through the glory of the Father,
so we too might walk in the newness of life.*

ROMANS 6:4

I'm Growing Up

PHOTO OF CHILD WHEN BOOK IS COMPLETED